Voyage of the Sable Venus and Other Poems

Voyage of the Sable Venus

AND OTHER POEMS

Robin Coste Lewis

ALFRED A. KNOPF   NEW YORK   2015

THIS IS A BORZOI BOOK
PUBLISHED BY ALFRED A. KNOPF

www.aaknopf.com/poetry

Knopf, Borzoi Books, and the colophon are registered trademarks of
Penguin Random House LLC.

Grateful acknowledgment is made to the following for permission
to reprint previously published material:

BOA Editions Ltd.: "a dream of foxes" from *The Collected Poems of Lucille Clifton,*
copyright © 1996 by Lucille Clifton. Reprinted by permission of The Permissions
Company, Inc. on behalf of BOA Editions Ltd., www.boaeditions.org.

Jean Valentine and Alice James Books: Excerpt from *Lucy: A Poem,* copyright © 2009
by Jean Valentine. Reprinted with permission of The Permissions Company, Inc.,
on behalf of the author and Alice James Books, www.alicejamesbooks.org.

Page 140 constitutes an extension of the copyright page.

Library of Congress Cataloging-in-Publication Data
Lewis, Robin Coste.
[Poems. Selections]
Voyage of the Sable Venus and other poems / Robin Coste Lewis.—First edition.
pages   cm
"This is a Borzoi book."
ISBN 978-1-101-87543-8 (hardcover)—ISBN 978-1-101-87544-5 (eBook)
I. Title.
PS3612.E98A6 2016
811'.6—dc23
2014047762

Jacket photograph: *Window Shopping* by Eudora Welty. Reprinted by permission of the
Mississippi Department of Archives and History and Russell & Volkening as agents for the
author. Copyright © by Eudora Welty, renewed by Eudora Welty, LLC.
Jacket design by Stephanie Ross

Manufactured in the United States of America
Published September 29th, 2015
Second Printing, October 2015

for

BEAUTY

Lucy
your secret book
that you leaned over and wrote just in the dirt—
Not having to have an ending
Not having to last

—JEAN VALENTINE

Contents

I

Plantation

And then one morning we woke up
embracing on the bare floor of a large cage.

To keep you happy, I decorated the bars.
Because you had never been hungry, I knew

I could tell you the black side
of my family owned slaves.

I realize this is perhaps
the one reason why I love you,

because I told you this
and you—still—wanted to kiss

me. We laughed when I said *plantation,*
fell into our chairs when I said *cane.*

There were fingers on the floor
and the split bodies of women

who'd been torn apart by horses
during the Inquisition.

You'd said, *Well I'll be damned!*
Every now and then you'd change

from a prancing black buck
into a small high yellow girl: pigtailed,

patent leather, eyes spinning gossamer, begging
for egg salad and banana pudding.

Or just as quickly you'd become
the girl's mother, pulling

yourself away from yourself.
Because my whole head was covered

with a heaving beehive, you thought
I didn't notice. I noticed. I cried honey.

And then you were fourteen, and you had grown
a glorious steel cock under your skirt. To brag

you rubbed yourself against me. Then your tongue
was inside my mouth, and I wanted to say

Please ask me first, but it was your
tongue, so who cared suddenly

about your poor manners?
We had books and a waterfall

was falling in the corner.
I didn't tell you I couldn't

remember what that thing was
you said to me once, that tender thing

you'd said I should never forget.
The moment you said it, I forgot it.

I wondered if you thought we were lost.
We weren't lost. We were *loss.*

And meanwhile, all I could think about
were the innumerable ways I would've loved

to have eaten you, how being
devoured can make one cry. And I hoped

you liked the fresh, pleasant taste
of juiced cane. You pulled

my pubic bone toward you. I didn't
say, *It's still broken;* I didn't tell

you, *There's still this crack.* It was sore,
but I stayed silent because you were smiling.

You said, *The bars look pretty, Baby,*
then rubbed your hind legs up against me.

On the Road to Sri Bhuvaneshwari

I.

Not much larger than a Volkswagen. Smiling
    on the dashboard: Gurumukh. Marigolds
        so mild we can chew. What we call *mountain*
            they say *foothill.* A whole vibrant green

valley of terraced balconies, rectangular
    rice farms carved into every façade
        for seven centuries. Now and then
            a clay road washed out by rain. We wait.

Barefoot men in madras dhotis, bodies
    large only as necessity, hoist twice that in boulders
        back up the mountain, back to that place
            where the road had been.

Monsoon. Uttar Pradesh. Twenty-eight days of rain.
    At dinner, someone says, During
        the nineteenth century, all this water
            caused the British to go

mad. They constantly committed suicide.
    Later, someone else
        points out their Victorian cemetery.
        I smile—a little.

That morning, seven langurs the size of six-
    year-olds, grey and brown, white and beige, tall tails
        curling, jumped up and down, shucked
            and jived on top of my cold tin roof.

Somehow, I am still alive.
        I know it is wrong
                to think of a decade as lost.
                        The more I recover, the more I go

blind. Squat
        naked beside a steaming bucket.
                Hold a small cloth.
                        In Trinidad, one says *clot.*

The *h* is quiet.
        A wafer of breath—just
                like here. There's no telling
                        what languishes inside the body.

Not mist, but a whole cloud
        passes into one window,
                then two hours later,
                        out the other.

The American college students try out
        their kindergarten Hindi: *ha-pee-tal,*
                ha-pee-tal. Lips finger the sign's script,
                        then the United States break

open their mouths
        into sad smiles when they realize
                it's not Hindi, but English
                        written in Devanagari: *hospital.*

For the whole day we drive
        along miles of wet, slithering clay
                to find a temple at the top of a *mountain*
                        where Shiva is said to have once dropped

a piece of Parvati.
        Every mountaintop made holy
                by the falling charred body part
                        of the Goddess. An elbow fell

here; here
>> fell Her toe; an ankle—black
>>> and burnt—Her knee. The road is wet and dark
>>>> red, and keeps spinning.

I sit behind the driver, admiring
>> his cinnamon fingers, his coiffed white beard,
>>> his pale pink turban wrapped so handsomely.
>>>> *Why did it take all that?*

I mean, why did She have to jump
>> *into the celestial fire*
>>> *to prove Her purity?*
>>>> *Shiva's cool—poisonous, blue,*

a shimmering galaxy—
>> *but when it came to His Old Lady,*
>>> *man, He fucked up!*
>>>> *Why couldn't He just believe Her?*

I joke with the driver. We laugh.
>> Gurumukh smiles back. But then I think, perhaps
>>> embodiment is so bewildering, even God grows
>>>> wracked with doubt.

For a certain amount
>> of rupees, the temple's hired a man
>>> to announce to tourists . . . *During the medieval period*
>>>> *virgins were sacrificed here.*

His capitalist glance mirrors our Orientalist tans.
>> *You're lying,* I say. *Save it*
>>> *for somebody pale.* He smiles, passes
>>>> me a bidi. I'm bleeding, but lie

so I can go inside and see
>> that burnt, charred piece
>>> of the Goddess that fell off
>>>> right here.

We climb up another one hundred
  and eight stairs. At the top, I try
    not to listen to anyone.
        An entire Himalayan valley. Chiseled.

Every mountain—peak to base—
  a terraced living verdant staircase
    for the Goddess to walk down:
      Sri Bhuvaneshwari.

II.

At night, our caravan winds back
  over gravel and clay. Ten headlamps
    grope the mountain walls
      of the green-black valley. The road

is only as wide as one small car. Hours of dog
  elbows, switchbacks, half roads.
    Slowly after a turn, the driver takes his foot
      off the gas, downshifts, coasts.

Black.   Warm.   Breath.   Snorting.
  Our car rubs against one biting grass off the face
    of a cliff. Then another, taller
      than our car. Then hundreds

block the road. Thick cylindrical horns scrape
  the driver's window; eyes so white, black
    pupils gleam, peering into our cab, grunting
      and drooling onto the window.

Now the whole car, surrounded. Warm black bodies
  covered in fur. Near their dusty hooves, children
    sit on the ground, nested in laps, quiet and smiling.
      Everyone embroidered with color:

silvers, metallic ochres, kohls, golds, reds, bold
        blacks, all of it—and a green so green
                I realize it's a shade
                        I have never seen.

A whole nomadic clan, traveling
        with hundreds of water buffalo. At least
                sixty human beings. There are so many
                        buffalo, our cars cannot move. And they can't move

the herd because a few feet ahead
        a She-Buffalo is giving birth.
                We get out.
                        And wait.

Out of habit, the students pull out their American sympathy,
        but then the driver says all the women sitting there
                on the ground, dusty, with children in their laps, dangling
                        their ankles over the mountain, adorned—all—

wear enough gold, own enough
        buffalo to buy your whole house—cash.
                The night holds. Life is giving birth
                        in the middle of a warm dark road.

Everyone in our party waits, smiling and gesturing
        with the whole clan, surrounded by snoring
                black bodies taller than our chins. We squat
                        beside their lanterns, stand inside our headlight.

The driver, who grew up in this valley,
        speaks two dialects, four national languages, plus English,
                cannot understand a single word anyone says.
                        Solid gold bangles, thick as bagels;

diamonds so large and rough they look
        like large cubes of clear glass. The women stare through
                their bright syllables. Then one lifts her hand, points
                        at one of us—says something—and they all laugh.

The calf is born dead. A folded and wet black nothing.
    It falls out of its mother—still—onto the ground.
        We watch it in the headlamps. Empty fur sack.
            A broken umbrella made of blood and bone.

The mother tries to run. Several men hold her, throw
    broad coils of ropes around her hooves. Two men, barefoot
        in dhotis, grab her on each side by her horns. And wait.
            They wait through her heaving. They sing

to her, they coo. Men who are midwives.
    Through four translations, they say it is her first time.
        She must turn around and see
            what has happened to her, or she will go mad.

We wait with the whole tribe, wait with the whole night, wait
    for her to stop bucking. Her hip bones
        are as tall as my eyes. Her neck is a massive drum.
            They do not force her, but they will not let her run.

She is pinned to the mountain, her black flat tail points down
    toward her dead newborn. There are four hands
        on her wide horns; four more hold the ropes
        surrounding her haunches.

Finally, after half an hour
    of bucking and grunting, she drops her eyes
        and gives. She lowers her face into it—into the black
            slick dead thing folded on the ground—

and sniffs. Nudges the body. Snorts.
    Then they let her go. She runs off, back
        into the snoring herd.
        Disappears.

One day, ten years later—one fine, odd day—suddenly
    I will remember all of this. That night, that dark
        narrow road will come back. Like a small sleepy child, it will sit
          gently down inside my lap and look up into me.

Kohl and camphor around all the babies' eyes
    to keep evil away; that exquisite smell of men
        and sweat and dust; the unanticipated calm
          of standing within

an enormous herd of sleeping water buffalo, listening.
    To spend your entire life—out of doors—walking the world
        with your whole family and neighborhood. To stay
          together, to leave together. *What a blessing,* I think,

and then, *What a curse!*
    My newborn is asleep in a red wagon
        that says *Radio Flyer.* I have packed
          a large suitcase and one box.

The World wants to know
    what I am made of. I am trying
        to find a way
          to answer Her.

I place our things by the door. And wait.
    Standing. Eyes closed. Looking. I want to
        remember the carved angels flying over the tall bay
          windows; the front door's twelve perfect squares

of beveled glass; the cloud-high ceilings;
    the baby's stuffed monkey; the tribal rugs; and the photograph
        of our tent in the desert that one soundless morning, on the floor
          of a canyon in Jordan. All in boxes now.

The lights are on. The house
            is empty. Night comes.
                        I smell the giant magnolia blossoms
                                    opening.

Once, I thought I was a person with a body,
            the body of something peering
                        out, enchanted
                                    and tossed.

The baby wakes. He is almost four
            weeks old. I give him a piece
                        of my body. He fingers my necklace
                                    strung with green glass beads.

I tie him onto my back and think about the brazen
            dahlias, nursed from seeds, staging a magenta riot now,
                        next to the rusty Victorian daybed, where he was conceived,
                                    beneath the happy

banana tree out on the back balcony.
            My father's gold earrings are welded into my ears.
                        My mother's diamonds are folded
                                    into a handkerchief inside my pocket.

And then, as if
            it is the most natural thing to do, I walk
                        toward the stairwell, and give
                                    the World my answer.

All the way down the staircase, my hand palms
            the mahogany rail, and I think, Once
                        this beam of wood stood high
                                    inside a great dark forest.

v.

Thick coat. Black fur. Two russet horns
          twisted to stone. One night
                   I was stuck on a narrow road,
                        panting.

I was pregnant.
          I was dead.
                   I was a fetus.
                        I was just born.

(Most days
          I don't know what I am).
                   I am a photograph
                        of a saint, smiling.

For years, my whole body ran
          away from me. When I flew—charred—
                   through the air, my ankles and toes fell off
                        onto the peaks of impassable mountains.

I have to go back
          to that wet black thing
                   dead in the road. I have to turn around.
                        I must put my face in it.

It is my first time.
          I would not have it any other way.
          I am a valley of repeating
                   verdant balconies.

Mother Church No. 3

KIN KLETSO/YELLOW HOUSE
CHACO CANYON, SAN JUAN COUNTY, NEW MEXICO
ANASAZI RUINS, AD 1125–1130

for Henri, at 2

You step down into the Flat World
Then ask me to say it, to explain

How our name can mean both *ancestor*
And *enemy.* Your body begins in four directions.

Here, one calendar takes eighteen years.
I am three. One day is an eyelash.

Your body is a segment of prehistoric road,
A buried stairwell with only the top stair obvious.

We are alluvial, obsidian.
Sometimes the ground swells

With disappointment; sometimes we know our mountains
Will be renamed after foreign saints.

We sing nine-hundred-year-old hymns
That instruct us in how to sit still

For forty-nine years
Through a fifty-year drought.

We climb down through the hole anyway,
And agree to the arrangement.

verga:

". . . women don't want the men to go
into the bush because the women
will only be raped but the men
will be killed . . . I have seen a woman who
was caught in the bush by several men.
They tied her legs to two trees while she
was standing. They raped her
many times and before leaving
her they put stones in her vagina . . ."

Abshiro Aden Mohammed, Kenya, 2000
Dagahaley Somali Refugee Camp
from *A Camel for the Son,*
by Fazal Sheikh

Before leaving her they put stones in her vagina
The men will only be raped but the stones will be killed
The bush caught many men to go into the stones
The stones will be killed by several trees before leaving
The bush tied the men to the trees in their vaginas
Before bush go to trees they kill many stones
Many men will be caught by the trees in the bush
Several trees will be raped by the bush and killed
Only the caught men will be stoned and bushed by the trees
Several men were caught by the trees before leaving
The men will be killed, but the stones will only be treed
The stones put many trees into the men's killed vaginas
By the bush, the trees were raped only several times
Before leaving, the vaginas were seen standing in the stones

The Wilde Woman of Aiken

ALBUMEN PHOTOGRAPH ON ORANGE MOUNT

J. A. PALMER, 1882

I am not supposed to be
beautiful. I am not
supposed to sit

before the observant eye
of a sunflower. I am incapable
of having a voice

like a robin's singing
of springtime's newborn impatiens,
its balsams and touch-me-nots

crouched so low to the ground.
Vases and I are not permitted
to dally. If I were a name,

it would be *Wall*
paper. My hair is made
of a million breathing paisleys.

For five thousand years,
I have listened to you
think aloud about a world

that does not exist.
I am sitting here,
in the open,

and you are there, dripping
beneath your dark
velvet, waiting for the light

to reach you.
I have wondered
where you really live,

why you cannot hear
all the glass inside your syllables
slide off the table

whenever your mouth
opens and is then closed.
The story has not even begun.

The only thing left inside
my hand is my own
quiet hand. I am the Fourth Sister.

My florets stand together
at golden angles. My head
is packed with eager seeds

crisscrossing in spirals
one hundred garlands long.
It's over now.

About my waist, dark
and bright, there is this
satin sash the color of sun

warmed eggplant
still fetching
on the vine.

You
cannot
prevent me.

The Mothers

We meet—sometimes—between the dry hours,
Between clefts in the involuntary plan,
Refusing to think of *rent* or *food*—how
Civic the slick to *satisfied* from *man.*

And democratic. A Lucky Strike each, we
Sponge each other off, while what's greyed
In and grey slinks ashamed down the drain.
No need to articulate great restraint,

No need to see each other's mouth lip
The obvious. *Giddy.* Fingers garnished
With fumes of onions and garlic, I slip
Back into my shift, then watch her hands—wordless—

Reattach her stockings to the martyred
Rubber moons wavering at her garter.

From:

To:

At last, a dark murderous lunatic
to whom they are allowed to respond.
Here, no one expects them to be strung
up by their necks—dangled—and then left

to be cut down from a tall tree—and not cry.
No law—here—will require them to watch
their families hurled on top of the world's bright pyre,
over generations—without complaint—

unattended by rage's holiness
or the clear mirror of grief. They find some
chalk to celebrate. While one loads, one lifts,
then checks. Just before they ignite the bomb,

they write on its shell—FROM HARLEM, TO HITLER—
then stand back for the camera, smiling.

Beauty's Nest

Beauty's nest
renders the body
mute. An elegance
so inconceivable,
it's violent. Extreme. It hurts
the heart to see
something so vast and deep
can also be made of dirt.

And if it can be
of the earth, the body
ponders, might
such a landscape
exist also within me?

The four of you stand
silent, uniformed on its rim,
while the imagination tries
to conceive all the things
it is still too dark
to see.

You jump back
into your wide tan Ford
and begin to drive
again—again—past
all the motels, and their signs,
which, were it not just
after midnight, you know—
and could see—say
WHITES ONLY

Red All Over

The politics of frogs
The musth of butterflies
Elegies of cotton
The whiteness of flies
Interruptions by snails
A lie's guarantee
The hope of succotash
A chorus of hominy
Permission of the persimmon
Observations by the spine
The pincushion's reassurance
The propaganda of a line
Cackling from the Bible
Orations by the dog
The mirror's steady rifle
The fig tree's scarlet log
Ands and their derision
Lending library in the eyes
Patois' agnosticism
The tongue's chain mail of whys?
Lady calling from the ocean
Invisible Man on the moon
Lindy-Hopping dead upon
The ceiling in the living room
Girl asleep in the avocado
The minstrelsy of the floor
Bickering Birds-of-Paradise
Picketing the fickle front door

Dog Talk

We-be   bo-broke   e-bev-ry-by
sy-byl-la-ba-ble-ble

O-bour   mo-bouths   bo-broke   the-bem
an-band   o-bo-pe-bened   the-bem
fo-bor   ai-bair   o-bor   wa-ba-ter-ber
o-bor   see-beed   o-bor   foo-bood.

A-banse-se-bers,   que-bues-tio-bens,
na-bames,   se-be-cre-bets.   We-be
be-bent   E-ben-gli-bish,
em-bem-bra-baced   i-bit
the-ben   e-be-ra-based   i-bit
a-bat   the-be   sa-bame   ti-bime.

Let Me Live in a House by the Side of the Road and Be a Friend to Man

I. HISTORIOGRAPHY

In their Heaven, God is a politician
who can't get enough votes
to be the Dog Catcher.

All the bodies we have
missed return, outlined
with fluorescent chalk.

The sun is a big green apple
dangling in a scarlet sky.
Masses of people bind themselves

up onto tall birch poles, to be
pecked at all day by anti-intellectual crows.
All the trash cans have saber teeth.

After school, they snatch and swallow
the slight bodies of brown boys.
If we make it there, our own kind points

us toward the sky's back door.
When we try to escape,
each taxi drives away

from our outreached hand,
suddenly off duty.

But in my Heaven,
there are five sparkling
Chrysler Buildings, and I take you

to the top of every one. God
is a melodramatic comedian who curses
just as elegantly as Richard Pryor.

The angels wear discarded clothes
made from painted and quilted dungarees.
They carry orange and yellow pom-poms

and know how to Cha-Cha. Deep
emerald rivers twist around this City—
not the East, nor the Hudson, but seven Mississippis.

In vacant lots, between
abandoned buildings, cornstalks
and sunflowers grow wild.

On Saturday nights, I make us
egg salad sandwiches, take out
the boat, then row and row.

There is a hurricane, inside
of which our whole world spins.
It's held within

the infinite palm
of a Goddess
who is Lena Horne's twin.

She wears a gossamer headdress,
and her raven-black tresses are plaited
with all the undiscovered galaxies.

And you—somehow you—
are skipping next to me
wearing a silver skirt,

click-clicking the whole way
in five-inch chrome pumps
made of plate glass.

We wonder together
about the history of history.
The Brooklyn Bridge is folded up

inside my pocket. Someday
I will put it on your finger
and beg you to marry me.

Between us, all the words I want
to say ricochet, exhausted, sweating.
When we stride down the street

the graffiti opens its large coffee eyes.
It follows our freckled footsteps—
and hangs there—quietly listening.

I am the Scarecrow, Tin Man, and Lion
combined. My head's a ticker tape of garbage,
I can't feel a thing, and I am terrified.

II. I.O.B.K. (INCAPABLE OF BEING KING)
SELF-PORTRAIT AS THE LION

for Ted Ross
(1934–2002)

inside a stone cast
peering out at the world
whirl by my heart
a bloody oyster brined
without artery or vein
arms crossed
outside the library
thinking up words all day
rarely confessing
the book's first physical duty
to be the mask
that hides the mane

III. SELF-PORTRAIT AS THE EMERALD CITY
NAIROBI, 2009

Is there a street that can anticipate
our tenderness? A corner or curb
that stands still waiting for me?

Where is the road—gilded and broad—
which can foresee our vast inability

not to love? A capital filled with small rivers
of gingered people sashaying silently through
the tinted streets, effortlessly unconcerned

with a certain world and the way it stares
into the mirror, admiring its own genitals.

Even if I were to disrobe and set out, humbly
whispering the questions of my life into my own ear,
I could not make it past the floor beside my bed

before my nakedness was offered as yet
further proof of our natal rage. I know

there are two presidents who seek solace
behind one enormous pewter mask: one
who believes in a verdant coup; the other

addicted to tradition's scarlet singe. I know
neither man has any real power. I know

one day they will become one man
only, and he will climb back up
into his wonderfully colored hot air

balloon and try to take this place with him.
I am tired. I want to leave. I want to believe

there is a room, a space, just one
ethereal molecule that finds delight
in its presumption of our delicate plainness.

There is yet any evidence, but people talk
about it: some odd empty place called *home*.

IV. GLINDA THE GOOD

for Lena Horne
(1917–2010)

Pray
there is something
like Her, something

hovering above us,
in whose palm
everything spins

Pray
the stars
are all the feelings

we refused to love
and somehow
they have forgiven us

our refusal
to address them
by their animal names

Summer

Last summer, two discrete young snakes left their skin
on my small porch, two mornings in a row. Being

postmodern now, I pretended as if I did not see
them, nor understand what I knew to be circling

inside me. Instead, every hour I told my son
to stop with his incessant back-chat. I peeled

a banana. And cursed God—His arrogance,
His gall—to still expect our devotion

after creating love. And mosquitoes. I showed
my son the papery dead skins so he could

know, too, what it feels like when something shows up
at your door—twice—telling you what you already know.

II

VOYAGE OF THE SABLE VENUS

And never to forget beauty,
however strange or difficult

—REGINALD SHEPHERD

The Metropolitan Museum of Art
Employees' Association Minstrel Show and Dance
will be held at the American Woman's Association
361 West 57th Street, Saturday evening,
October 17, 1936

I am anxious to buy a small healthy negro girl—
ten or twelve years old, and would like to know
if you can let me have one . . .

—MRS. B. L. BLANKENSHIP

The Ship's Inventory:

Four-Breasted Vessel, Three Women
in Front of a Steamy Pit, Two-Faced
Head Fish Trying on Earrings, Unidentified.

Young Woman with Shawl
and Painted Backdrop, Pearl
of the Forest, Two Girls

with Braids People
on a Ship with Some Dancing
Girls. Our Lady of Mercy, Blue.

Nude Iconologia Girl
with Red Flower Sisters
of the Boa Woman Flying a Butterfly.

Kite   Empty
Chair   Pocket
Book   Girl

in Red Dress with Cats and Dog's Devil.
House Door of No Return. Head-of-a-Girl-
In-the-Bedroom in the kitchen.

Contemplation Dark-Girl Girl.
In the Window Negress with
Flower Sleeping Woman

(Negress with Flower Head
of a Woman-Nude in a Land
scape)—Libyan Sybil: Coloured, Nude-High

Yellow Negro Woman
and Two Children—The Flight
of the Octoroon: the Four Quarters of

the World, Holding
a Celestial Sphere.

Invocation

BLESSING THE BOAT

Untitled
Anonymous
Clay

Prehistoric
Cow
Bone

Detail

Of a
Balsarium
Glass Moss

Fragment
Untitled Gelatin
Silver Print

On Paper On
Stucco On Canvas
On Concrete

Apotheosis:

> *Obverse anthropomorphic sarcophagus.*
> *Alabastron eulogia ampulla.*

> *Anonymous fragment.   Frag*
> *Ment.   Pavement (Detail).   Pain t*

> *On tin—Figure 150, Figure 151:*
> *Strings and black mud.*

> *Terracotta terracotta.*
> *Anonymous relief.*

Untitled Anonymous Limestone,
Isolated Ronde Bosse.

Plant Fiber Beads, Red
Abrus Seeds, Solar-Mosaic Wood Plate.

Ointment Vase, Printed Bedspread,
Artificial Hair—Neck

Decoration from a Tunic. Untitled Chewing Gum,
Gold—Gold Repoussé, Anonymous Plaster-Ink.

Salted Paper, Coins, Carbon,
Ivory-Colored Pencil. Graffiti

On the sides and undergirding
Of a bridge. Da Guerre!

O Type accumulated—Figurine 38 felt
Tip monumental relief.

Grass	*Stain*
Ivory	*Spoon*
Berry	*Juice*
White	*Pigment*

Hide.

Heads and Busts
Headless—Footless—Armless

But with a Strongly
Incised Vaginal

Opening:

Harp

Harp
With Bridge   *Harp*
Lute

One-key
Xylophone
Slit

Gong
Trumpet   *Gong*
Gong

Mallet
Whistle
Rattle

Drum

Catalog 1:

ANCIENT GREECE & ANCIENT ROME

Here is your name
said the woman
and vanished in the corridor
—MAHMOUD DARWISH

I.

Statuette of a Woman Reduced
to the Shape of a Flat Paddle

Statuette of a Black Slave Girl
Right Half of Body and Head Missing

Head of a Young Black Woman Fragment
from a Statuette of a Black Dancing Girl

Reserve Head of an African Princess
Statuette of a Concubine

Full Length Figure of a Standing
Black Woman Wearing Earrings

Statuette Once Supported an Unguent Vase
Vase with Neck in the Form of a Head

of a Black Statuette of a Female
Figure with Negroid Features

Figure's Left Arm Missing Head
of a Female Full-length Figure

of a Nubian Woman
the Arms Missing

Bust of a Draped Female Facing Forward
One Breast Exposed   Black

Adolescent Female with Long Curls and Bare
Breasts Wearing a Voluminous Crown

Partially Broken Young Black Girl
Presenting a Stemmed Bowl

Supported
by a Monkey

:

Standing Female Reliquary Figure
with Crested Coiffure and Hands

Clasped in Front of Torso, Holding
a Staff Surmounted by a Human Head

Figure Has Prominent
Vagina Bended

Knees and Oversized Head
with Half-Open Eyes

and Semicircle Mouth
That Juts Out

from the Face Some
Fine Scarification

on Chest and Belly
Dark Brown Almost Black

Patina with Oil Oozing
in Several Places

Numerous Cracks
on Back of Head and Hole

on the Coiffure
One Nipple Appears

to Be Shaved Off
or Damaged Black Woman

Standing on Tiptoe
on One End of a Seesaw

While a Caricatured Figure Jumps
on the Other

End

[Two Nubian Prisoners Bound
to a Post] Protome [Probably

the Handle of a Whip
or Other Implement] Oil Flask Back

View Head of an African Prisoner
Statue of Prisoner Kneeling Arms

Bound at the Elbows
Left Arm Missing

Bust of a Nubian Prisoner
with Fragmentary Arms

Bound Behind Funerary Mask
of a Negro with Inlaid Glass Eyes

and Traces of Incrustations
Present in the Mouth

Censer in the Form of a Nude Negro
Dwarf Standing with His Hands

at His Sides upon an Ornate Tripod
and Supporting on His Head

a Small Cup
in the Shape

of a Lotus
Flower

water jar

bowl

ointment spoon

in the form of swimming
black girl

mirror
with handle

in the form of a carved standing
black girl

handle
of a sistrum

a Bes and an Isia dancing
back-to-back

two nails

with Negro heads in relief

head

of a Negro which may have adorned

a pin

mounted in a

ring

bezel

bowl

                                        decorated with three heads
                                        in relief

                                        separated by flat veined leaves
                                        female puppet with

mortar and pestle
necklace

                                        with two heads
                                        of black women forming

a clasp
perfume vase

                                        head of an adolescent

aryballos

                                        juxtaposing two heads of Negroes
                                        cast from the same mold

mirror
with handle

                                        in the form of a young Nubian
                                        female standing

lamp

                                        in the form of

the head

                                        of a black perhaps

incense
shovel

                                        with a Negro head attached

to handle
a girl

                                        with long corkscrew curls
                                        round face wide
                                        flat nose and mouth

open

                                        and jutting forward
                                        to form

a spout

inkwell

                                        in the form of a crouching
                                        Negro Negro
                                        seated writing on

a scroll

IV.

Standing

Female Figure with Child Kneeling
Female Figure with Child Standing
Female Figure Head
Rest Supported by Seated
Female Figure Kneeling
Female Figure with Bowl Standing
Female Figure with Bowl and Child Standing
Female Figure Seated
Female Figure (Pipe)
Female Figure Undated
Female Figure Mask
Female Rhythm Pounder

Standing

v.

Attendants bringing
Offerings to the burial

Funerary relief
Detail of relief

Carved relief
Grave relief

Vase with painted
Decoration relief

Site relief
Relief fragment

From the tomb (Isis
Receiving the Sacrifice)

Relief
Relief

Relief
Relief

Catalog 2:

VI.

A slave carries jar and two dead birds.
Another slave who carries three

fish and a sheaf of wheat
enters a tower.

Askos, a black woman dancing
between a maenad and a satyr, black dancer

beside a woman playing a tabor—
sacred dance performed

during an Isiac Ceremony, Negroid
dancers and musicians overall.

View: a juggler, a black dancer, Female
Offering Bearer Young Female Slave

with Negroid features carrying a stool mask
of a woman shown holding pouch and basket—

or urn—above two geniuses holding garland.
A standing figure of a Laughing Person

wearing a short tunic with large broad nose, thick
lips, and both male and female attributes: his right

arm broken off at the elbow, the left
arm missing completely.

VII

THE QUEEN HAS HER HAIR DONE

Attendants with jewelry, sun shades,
and a mirror, move from right to left.

Mask of a Woman with a large coil
of Plaited Hair Mask of a Woman

with her hair in a Small Knot Mask
of a Woman with Her Hair Rolled

at the Forehead and Temples Mask
of a Woman with Austere Hair Style Mask

of a Woman with Radiating Waves of Hair.
Small and Magical Stela Anhydrite Mummy Mask

of a Woman with a Jeweled Garland Shroud Bracelet
richly adorned diadem with rosette gold

and in lay Two Linen Marks from the Tomb
of a Tattooed Woman Sporting Boat

A Cleopatra holding a—?
Cornucopia Attendants moving

from left to right linen,
from mummy-wrapping Aphro

Dite rising from the bath.   I Sis Aphro
Dite clasping a garment

rolled about her hips:
The Place of Silence

VIII.

lotus leaves
buds and cornflowers

poppies and grapes
shape and size of relief

raise their arms
dance on tiptoe

in the tomb

in the relief

a little girl sings
with musicians playing

percussion instruments
the floor sweeper leans

his broom against his skirt
in order to free his arms

for prayer

the curve

of the sandaled feet
vividly conveys

the excitement
of the event

:

head of a princess

with alterations

the small relief

a young gazelle

on the arm of a princess

the relief at bottom

a bull

(ially preserved   )

is led

place

offering   partly damaged

relief in the Center

the beautifully carved torso

The Queen, Who

Her Arms

the food

Piled   a table

part   the relief

        the Center

:

small relief

in the   from   bottom

shows portion

Lady-in-Waiting

ing   translucent

breasts

her right hand is a scarf

feather fan

commonly

royal

two heads

the uppermost relief left

end of   representation

:

                    Angles

        a room   like   heads

                upper most   the two

partly

            small relief

(*disk*) -shaped

        adorning

                        worn

        women

Occasion

                    glories   poppies

            cornflowers

IX

"Her head is that of a Lioness"

"The short mane of a feline . . ."

"The disk on Her head identifies her

as the Daughter of the Sun . . ."

"King Amenhotep III commissioned hundreds

of statues of the Goddess for his mortuary temple in western Thebes."

". . . brought to England in early 1800s . . ."

". . . these statues were exhibited in the recesses of Waterloo Bridge . . ."

". . . and later by Lord Amherst on the terrace

of his country house."

x.

South Wall

> *". . . to your beautiful face"*

North Wall

> *"life, all happiness, all food, all provisions"*

West Wall

> *". . . as long as the sun exists, your name will exist . . ."*

Catalog 3:

XI. GARDEN OF EARTHLY DELIGHTS CLASS IN ANCIENT HISTORY

Rainy-Night Sarah
is brought to Pharaoh.

Pharaoh gives Sarah back
to Abraham—Wild Men

and Moors. Melancholy Moses
fighting in the Land of the Blacks

where he finds a wife, historiated.
Bible between two captives, three fates:

Fontana dei Quattro Mori Group
of the Elect Group of the Damned.

A god on the left, a prince
on the right. Back to Back

Solomon worshipping idols, black
laborers on the quays

of Venice. Black African figure
at the edge of the canal, miracle

at the Bridge of San Lorenzo, O Lymp!
I, a miracle of the Black-Leg-Birth of the Virgin,

The Black Bride of the Song of Songs—
Black African Diana the Good

Woman of Color Saint Lucy Before
the Magistrate, Pregnant

Eva the First
Lady

Chapel of the Miraculous Image
Inside the Gates of Dawn—

Nigra Sum Sed Formosa Church
of the Black Madonna:

Madonna of Succor
Our Lady of Crea

Our Lady of Peace
and Good Voyage Tanned

Madonna Black Madonna
Madonna Bruna

Black Virgin Dark Madonna
Our Most

Holy
Mother of God

: *Assumption Immaculata Perpetual Virginity Black Chapel Mother,*
The Enslavement of Our Lady the Tabernacle Woman of Revelation,
Queen of Heaven of God, Miracle Mother-Mother of God—Patroness,
Your Majesty Virgin of the Miracle Church of the Black Madonna

Our Lady
of Presentation

Our Lady
of the Confession

Our Lady
of the Rule

Our Lady
of Plain Light

Our Lady
of the Castle

Our Lady
of the City

Our Lady
of the Hermits

Our Lady
of the Visitation

Our Lady
of the Pillar

—in Vilnius Lithuania   —Romería de la Virgen   —Senhora Aparecida

—Olho D'água São João Maria   —de Belloc à Dorres—

—de Montgrony   —La Virgen Negra Istenanya de Montserrat

(in Halles-Sous-les-Côtes)   —de Pompéia   —del Pinar

Black Mary Magdalene of Palestine

Black Madonna Czestochowa, Queen of Poland

Catalog 4:

XIV.

Gone!
An Historical Romance of Civil War as It Occurred
Between the Dusky Thighs of a Young Negress and Her Heart Detail

(From a Series of the Four Continents Allegory of America, or Parajba en Brasil—
Israel in Egypt—View of Rio de Janeiro from the Hills)

Mil Años de Creatividad:

        Alabama Sketchbook:
        Seated Negro Woman Looking
        to the left, drawing

        half-length image
        of a Young Negro Woman
        Wearing a Dress with an Empire.

        Waistline and pearl,
        earrings and necklace, and holding
        a basket of flowers over her left arm, painting

        The Slaves escaping through
        the swamp, The Slave watching
        her pursuers in for e—

Ground Black Woman walking in front
of a Board Fence Background Plantation House
and Outbuildings (or Slave Quarters).

In a Grove of Trees Slave Woman wearing a Runaway.
Collar with Two Children, emaciated.
Negro Man eating Dead.

Horseflesh in the background.
Negro Man strapped to a ladder, Being.
Lashed Slave Woman seen

from the back, her head in left
profile, kneading bread and smoking
a Pipe Parrot Vendor Negress.

Carrying Her Young Slave Woman
carrying Baby and Negro Boy, running.
At Left Negro Man at right, Being.

Held by the collar, two dogs wear
collars, one labeled "Cass,"
the other: "Expounder."

:

The Negro Revenged Negro Man on a Precipice
calling down Nature's Fury on a slave.

Ship Negro Woman seated.
At right, Slavers throwing over.

Board the Dead-and-Dying.
Typhoon coming.

On manacled limbs of
Slaves among the Waves:

Foreground-Slave,
Ship in Middle

Distance: a Black Woman Kneeling
in a Storm, Her Hands Clasped

in Prayer and Her Eyes
Cast Upward.

Nude Black Woman
in an Oyster Shell

Drawn by Dolphins
through the Water

and accompanied by Cupids,
Neptune, and Others.

:

American Gothic Colored Individuals
Along the Road Side Slave Woman with a Chain
On Her Wrist Kneeling Beside Abraham Lincoln
Who Points Toward Items on a Chair

A Woman and Her Dog in the Window
Black Girl Seated on Watermelon
And Holding a Bottle of Ginger
And Baby in Watermelon Crib

Black Girl Standing
Behind Her
A Redeemed Slave Child
Slave Pen

Two Black Overseers
Flogging Two Negro Slaves
One a Nude Man Suspended from a Tree
The Other a Woman

Bared to the Waist and Tied
To a Tree as a White Woman
Observes Head and Shoulders
Of a Slave Woman Seen in Left Profile

A Standing Female Slave Nude to the Hips
With Manacles on Her Wrists
Holding Up a Drapery
And Looking Downward

:

A Negro Slave Woman
Carrying a Cornucopia
Representing Africa

A Negro Slave Woman
Holding a Plate of Tropical Fruits
Including a Pineapple

A Negro Servant Boy
Brings in a Tray
Of Filled Glasses Winged

Female Figure of Hope
Leaning
On an Anchor

And Holding a Wreath
Over an Inscribed Monument
With a Bale of Cotton

And a Ship
In the Background Negro Boy
Holding Feathers in His Left Hand

Pointing to Hope
And a Book
Under His Right Arm

And a Black Man
Holding a Rifle
And Pointing to the Arms

Of the United States
Above to Their Side
Is a Ballot

Box and Behind
Them a Loco
Motive

:

At Auction Negro Man in Loincloth
serves liquor to Men Bidding

on The Slaves while A Slave Woman
attends Two Women Observing The Sale.

African Slave Encased in an Iron Mask
and Collar Slave Children starting out

to harvest coffee on an oxcart.
Negroes under a date palm.

Negro Woman Seated
at a table, facing

left, writing
with a quill.

:

Abraham Lincoln holding
a Kneeling Black Woman

by the wrist
and lifting Her

to Her Feet
Charity Holding

Three Children
one White one Red one Black

with a Chinese Holding
Her Drapery

Kneeling Negro Woman
lifting Her Fettered Hands

in Supplication to a Female Figure
Personifying Justice

Inside a Wreath
Negro Woman and White Woman Shaking

Hands Negro Man and White Man
His Arm

Around a Small Negro Girl
Doing the Same

Inside a Wreath of Sugar
Cane Stems

:

The Mulatress African Woman with Basket Kongo Basket
full of fruit, diamond-sluicing the Drake Jewel ('Laud

Anum!) Aspiration: the Masque of Blackness—
Work on Progress into Bondage.

Tall Figure Lilith, The Goat Tender of the Colonies,
(A Christmas Gift to Ole Marster and Missus):

"Merry Christmas and Christmas Gift, Ole Massa!"
A Black Child Wearing

Broken Chains
And Blowing Him

A Kiss

When the Woman's Left Ear
Ring is Pulled

Her Eyes Recede
And a Mechanism Rises

Into Place
Showing the Hour

In the Right Eye
And Minutes

In the Left
The Right Earring

Was Originally
Designed

To Release
A Musical

Movement
With the Pipe

Organ
In the Base

:

Negro Woman Holding
A Bow and Arrow and Wearing

A Quiver
Sits on the Movement

Of the Table Clock at Her Feet, a Turtle
To Her Side a Female Lion

Base Decorated with a Black
Hunting and Fishing

:   *"L'Effroi" (The Terror) Full-Length*

Figure of a Negro Woman
Holding

Her Child Over
Her Head

Out of Reach
Of a Serpent

Climbing Up
Her Dress

Catalog 5:

EMANCIPATION & INDEPENDENCE

XVI.

A Nun Embracing a Girl
         In a Doorway   Water Dancing
                  Girl
                        Girl Carrying Child

Wrapped in Blanket on Back
         With Two Girls Near
                  Dance Rock Girl
                           Nearby Girl

Near Well Girl
         Who Stays Home Woman
                  Brushing
                           Girl's Hair

:

Portrait [Front]
　　　of Group of Women
　　　　　from Montana
　　　　　　　Left to Right

Good Road Girl
　　　Mrs. Red Dog Grows in Bed
　　　Old Woman
　　　　　　Fierce Woman and Dove

All in Native Dress
　　　The Question Mark Girl
　　　　　Girl Singing in the Wreckage
　　　　　Girl in Native Dress

On Horseback Four Women
　　　and One Girl All in Blankets
　　　　　on Side of Street Near Wood Frame
　　　　　Buildings

:

Portrait
    of General L. W. Colby
        of Nebraska State Troops
           Holding

Baby Girl
    Zintkala Nuni
        (Little Lost Bird) Found
           on Wounded Knee

Battlefield
    South
        Dakota
           1890

:

Girl Tending a Cow
        Black Girl from the Cottingham Suite
                Girl Writing a Letter
                        Girl in Partial Native Dress

With Ornaments:
        Black Seeds Calla Lilies
                Cyclamen Red
                        And Yellow Flowers

Little Girl in Orange
        Black Girl White Flower
                Black Girl Dragging White Girl
                        Blue

Girl Behind Black Door
        Black Forest Girl
                Girl in a Green Dress
                        Half-Length Portrait of a Mulatto Girl

Wearing
        A Madras Tignon
                And Pearls Girl
                        In Church Girl

In Front of Chalkboard Girl
        Talk Girl
                Walking Girl
                        Jumping

Rope
        In Maryland Park Girl
                Carding Wool Girl
                        Jumping

Rope
          Head and Shoulders Girl
                    Portrait of an Unidentified Girl
                              Young Black Girl

from Copiapó, Chile
          Winnebago Girl
                    Washing Clothes in a Stream
                              Seated Girl with Legs Folded

"Miss Girl" Peasant Girl
          Negro Girl
                    Nude Reclining on Couch Girl
                              on Oriental Rug Street of the Slave Girls

Literary and Industrial Training School
          for Negro Girls
                    A Section of the Girls
                              of the Senior Class

Taking
          a Course in Woodworking
                    Negro Career Girl
                              Ladies' Whipping Girls

Negro Girl Pelted by Crowd
          Potholders
                    with Black Boy and Girl
                              Eating Watermelon

Young Girl
          with Red, Black, and Green
                    Flag Girl
                              from Sene   Gal

Little Brown Girl
          Girl Standing in a Tree
                    First Day of Voluntary
                              School Integration

Lone Black Girl on School Bus
in Milwaukee, Wisconsin
Head of a Girl Wearing an Ornate Head

Dress

XVII

Scene 60 Blockade
    Rue de la Lyre
        Outside, Day:

Moorish Women
    On their way
        To the cemetery

Moorish Women
    On their way
        To a marabout

Moorish Women Taking
    A Walk Moorish
        Women in Town

Attire Moorish
    Woman in City
        Attire Kabyl Woman

Covering herself
    With the haik. Aicha
        And Zorah Moorish

Woman at Home
    I am sending you a package
        To be picked up

At the railway station.
    Ouled Nayl
        Woman Uled Nayl.

Young Beduin
    Woman Moorish
        Woman from Laghuat

Moorish Woman Pouring
     Her Kaoua Moorish
          Woman Smoking

A hookah:
     Bon Souvenir Natives
          in their quarters reclining.

Odalisque Dance
     Of the Almehs. Belly
          Dancing the Dance-Dance

Of the Veil Dance.
     Don't get bored Dance.
          Moorish Woman at Home.

Moorish Women
     In their Quarters Beautiful
          Fatmah at Home

In Full Regalia Woman
     From the South Kabyl Woman
          Woman from the Far South

Of the Oran District Moorish
     Woman from Constantine
          Young Woman from the Algerian

South *Oh*
     Is it ever hot!
          Moorish Bust

The Cracked Jug in Contemplation
     (les secrets de l'histoire
          naturelle contenant les merveilles

et choses memorable du monde—
     L'emancipazione dalla schiavitu),
          La Danse African in Algerian Costume—

Nègre du Tombouctou,
    Nègre du Soudan, ou
        Nègre en Costume.

XVIII.

THE SWEET FLYPAPER OF LIFE VIRGIN ON THE ROCKS
DETERMINING TRUE NORTH IN THE RAIN

The Bather Octoroon Woman on Giraffe-
    Skin breast-feeding the Mulatress.

Untitled Family Negro House along fence.
    The Blind Woman Liberty displaying the Arts

and Sciences City of the Dead. Uncle Ned's
    School ' Emancipated Slaves Eel-Spearing at Setauket.

The massacre at New Orleans Cotton Pickers'
    visit from the Old Mistress guest at dinner.

The Indian Widow Phrenological Head,
    an Indian maiden-spirit of the dead, washing clothes.

Forever Free Anonymous Portia ironing.
    Untitled Woman at a gate, holding a cat.

Pictures of Southern life: prawn-fishing mummers
    and carnival crowd walking outside on the street.

Day-Work-Woman scrubbing Aunt Dicy,
    Woman-of-the-Tobacco-Madonna-of-the-Field.

Jubilee Maternal Recruiter sitting at table interviewing
    Family Female Convicts seated outside Sing Sing Prison.

I'm-Just-Doing-My-Job-Red-Cross-Nurses handing out
    wool for knitting Free-Fall Female Atrocity Victim.

Watching, ex-voto: Miracle of Our Lady
    of the Rosary Off the Coast of Brazil

(Float carries The Queen of Strife and is decorated
          with cast flowers and depiction of two twisted bodies).

In came a storm of wind, rain, and spray—
          weary and dissatisfied with everything.

All-Coons-Look-Alike-to-Me
          men and women carrying bricks.

Massacre of Whites by Indians and Blacks in Florida.
          The Mourners bench progress of the American Negro.

The Hampton Albums water, color-studying the butterfly.
          The Old Arrow Maker and his daughter, Untitled Negro Woman,

Building-More-Stately-Mansions Study Hour.
          Rise, shine, for thy time has come, Negro Woman:

An Untitled American Family Interdenominational Chapel.
          Untitled Young Negro Girl wearing long dress

and bonnet, standing in field holding flowers.
          Anonymous Reclining Negress Woman, at rest

(by candlelight-memory)
          in the garden.

Catalog 6:

XIX.

Anonymous speaking at memorial for Four Negro Girls
killed in church bombing in Birming.   Ham.

President Kennedy addressing the crowd: A Red *Boo*!
A Negro *Boo*! Young Girls being held

in a prison cell at the Leesburg
Stockade. Wounded, civil.

Rights demonstrators in the hospital
and on the street-burned-out-bus:

Bronzeville Inn Cabins for Coloreds. Here lies
Jim Crow drink Coca-Cola white.

Customers
Only!

:

Birth Treat Girl in Red,
The Two Paths:
What will The Girl become?

Preparing for school
and canvassing for votes:
The Breck Girl The New Black

South Uptown Woman
Scolding Her Companion Woman
Leaning on Radio Woman

Selling Earrings
in Front of Car Woman
with Laundry Bag on Top of Head

Two Negro Girls playing
with yarn and knitting
Needle at Harlem Playground

Three Negro Teenage Girls modeling
clothing for the Teen-Age Consumer
A-Go-Go Woman Holding Up

Spoon at Boy with Mask
who is scaring Young Girl
Negro Woman Peeling

Potatoes Girl in Dress with White Collar
New Jerusalem Women's Rifle Team
at Howard University Integration

Crisis Woman and Daughter
with Children and 22 Million
Very Tired and Very Angry People

Women Marching
in Front of White House,
Crows Wait

Along the Funeral Route
Dancehall Queen Doing the Chaplin
Down the Flank

:

Anonymous Do Drop Inn
Blessed Sun Bathing Negress
Rent Day Beauty in the slums—

Clapping Christening Cleaning
Club Women Cooking Class
at the Benjamin Banneker!

The Green Chair People in a line.
Queens of the Boat hear animals dancing,
wrapping it up at the Lafayette:

Wannabes at the White Party
Gold Brick Inn Roseland
Asphalt Jungle.

Female Carnival Ride Primitive Girl,
The Boss pulling your own strings.
Humanity Servant, you're fine, you're hired.

Group Portrait in the Dark Tower:
Picture perfect painted toenails colonnade—
The Annotated Topsy Series, Untitled,

The Cow Jumped Over the Moan.
Let by gones be bygones, Hiawatha Woman
with Jug Grievin' Hearted Full Blown Magnolia,

measuring and pacing Playland—Comrades!
The Sun God and the Poet
swinging in the park.

There were Colored People there:
In the background, The Pimp—
God's Gift–to–Man

(He told her he wanted to
talk to her and she told him
he could talk all he wants to—).

Clara Mae angry
at Her Sister
and Her Husband.

Workers take the lead,
Midnight Benefit Show: The Screw
as Applied to the Cheese Press.

Me and Willie Mae, Ram Man, Tom Boy,
Moose Lady with a gentleman named Charles Bailey,
Models displaying printed leather shoes.

Tom Boy, Love Owl, Five Sorcerers, Seven
Faces of Eve—Little Miami Magic
People. On Such a Night as This

Unidentified Man Woman and Cat,
Unidentified Something
That Ain't Been Born Yet.

Woman Power!
She's Black, She's Beautiful
She's Smart, She's Registered

She'll Vote.
How about You?
Now Dig This:

Don't Hate Me
Because I'm Beautiful
Untitled.

Somebody Paid the Price
for Your Right.
Register to Vote!

(You Don't Bomb the People)
You Can *Register Now*!
No Reading or Writing

Necessary
Thenceforward
And Forever

Free—*Thought*
You Might Enjoy This
Memento of the Occasion!

Catalog 7:

MODERN POST

XX.

Landscape, Western Hemisphere (le tumulte noir)

Spiral arteries in the female body, evidence
of accumulation, empirical construction extending
horizontal form. Delirium wake and resurrection,

landscape allegories, suprematist evasion,
Black City Convalescents from Somewhere.
My irony surpasses all

Others. Have you any flesh
coloured silk stockings, young man?
Still   Life   Wild   Fowl

Death-Witness while you wait.
I embody everything you most hate
and fear: African   African't   an An

Ti-Slavery Meeting Black Tie Cement Ball:
An Opera in Three Acts.
I have special reservations

between me and the rest
of the land there are bars, something
brown, carmine, & blue:

Middle Grey Grey Area—
Greenheads-Brownheads Untitled Brigade
(stadia circulation style in spades!)

Retopistics Troubled Island,
Zero-Canyon typology.
Do you think

A is *B*?   *Girl/Boy?*
Red-Ball Slave-Girl in holiday attire,
Slave-Girl-with-Jade-Doves-Comb-with-Birds

(Phoenix Segregation). Enough
reframing the past—I sell the shadow
to support the Substance Runway.

:   *Dick-and-Jane-with-Me Page Spread*
      The Upper Room II Flipside Self

Untitled Female Drinker Figure—
Reclining Silent Protest Parade.
The result of the Fifteenth Amendment Ritual
and Revolution Self Possession.

Invisible Black Russians—girls with guns—
(Lenin watched from the Tower).
This is my life, cutting up
old film. Don't edit

the wrong thing out
Untitled World's Exhibition: Being
the Narrative of a Negress
in the Flames of Desire

(What remains inside
Pandora Mechanical Girl?
Rabbithole? Fingerprints?
Secrets, Tales

of Amnesia?). I see it
every day, The Conscience
of the Court: Woman-in-Interiors, Plate 1
Wedding Night Untitled Venus

looking into the mirror,
the Black Woman asked
"Mirror, Mirror on the wall,
who's the finest of them all?"

The Mirror says,
"Snow White
you Black Bitch,
and don't you forget it,

Sphinx!"

:   *Las Meninas Autoportrait:*
    As Armas do Império

Untitled Anonymous Memory
(the Shape of Things)
Old Dog New Trick Boo

Hoo Revisionist Liberation,
Monkey May Flower May Days
Dawn of Ann: The Liberation
of Aunt Jemima Dancing at the Louvre!

Anonymous Mademoiselle Bourgeoise Noire
celebrates with her friends: I'll Be
a Monkey's Uncle Untitled Committee
to Defend the Panthers Anonymous Fairy Godmother

offers some unrequested advice,
letter from a black girl: Free Black
and passive-aggressive

without sanctuary.

:   *Self-Portrait in Studio*
(Courtesy of The Artist)
The Upper Room I

My grandmother and aunts
Outside of church, Sisters of the Holy
Family. Three seated figures, guarded

Conditions: Firefighter, firebirds, light
In the window—portrait with sunflowers—
Nine-Lives Pageant of Birds
Torchy in heartbeats.

Anonymous homage to an Unknown
Suburban Black Girl. Self-Portrait
With Mingus Helmet Mask:

Untitled Self-Portrait Spirit
Untitled Book Page
Untitled Woman in a Sardine

Can Emerging, Rocking
Mary Woman Wearing a Fish
Hat. Blackware Pot Maiden,
Fétiche et fleurs, lay on top of me.

Untitled Woman laying down.
Anonymous touching her

Breast.

Darkytown Rebellion
Tit for Tat Brooch

Cut—Beat—Burn—
Balance—Consume

The Rich Soil Down There,
The Bush-Shinn Deboning.

You don't know where
her mouth has been!

Blackberry Woman, Seated
(woman in a blue and black dress),

Stars and Fireworks Woman
Feeding Bird Woman, brushing hair.

Bathsheba at the Fountain,
Venus Before a Mirror

(three wishbones
in a wooden box).

Hip-Hip Hooray! Look Away!
Look Away! Look Away!

"They was Nice
White Folks

While They
Lasted"

(Says One Gal
to Another).

D-Man in the water, *Pomo-Afro-Homo* Peacock
of the Sea, the Spirit of the Dead, watches the Message:

Paris is burning the white to be angry, Anonymous.
Your *kunst* is your *waffen,* Anonymous.

Untitled tongues untied, Untitled American
Gothic marginal eyes, still/here, looking

for Langston. The Black Birds on a steamboat,
Guardians of Desire, the singing head:

*Where Do We Come From—What Are We—
Where Are We Going?*—Blues.

Black Girl in a stream,
The Waving Girl seen

from anatomies of escape.
Home by dark, over her *le Cake.*

Walk (Economical Love Pussy Control)!
Tous les soirs Les Zoulous, Stargazer!

What on Earth have you done
to this coffee, Black Blossom?

*Pour vous, Madame,
Paso doble* as I am.

The Aftermath: underwear
window-shopping, Sunday

morning, fireflies
on the water, blue shade—

Silence.
Poise. Prayer:

Tinted Venus

African Venus

Dolni Vestonice

Magdalenian Venus

Ram Mal'ta Venus

Venus from Laugerie-Basse

Venus of Hohle Fels

Venus of Monruz

Venus of Willendorf

Venus of Berekhat

Venus of Lespugue

Venus of Hradok

Venus of Tan-Tan

(Thirteen ways of looking at a black girl)

:

I send you these few lines in order

To bring you up

On what has been

Happening to me.

—Venus of Compton

(Young Woman and Hope, Holding
Photo of Pearl)

Catalog 8:

Still:

Life

(of Flowers)

with Figures—

including

a Negro servant.

Notes

Art hurts.
Art urges voyages—
—GWENDOLYN BROOKS

BAYERISCHES NATIONALMUSEUM, MÜNCHEN

HENRY FRANCIS DU PONT WINTERTHUR MUSEUM, WINTERTHUR, DELAWARE

NATIONAL ACADEMY OF DESIGN, NEW YORK, 1860

MUSÉE DES BEAUX-ARTS DE LA VILLE DE PARIS

STAATLICHE MUSEEN ZU BERLIN, ANTIKENSAMMLUNG (PERGAMONMUSEUM)

MISSOURI HISTORICAL SOCIETY

NATIONAL MUSEUM OF VICTORIA, MELBOURNE REPOSITORY

LIBRARY OF CONGRESS, PRINTS AND PHOTOGRAPHS DIVISION, WASHINGTON, DC

MUSEUMS AT STONY BROOK

MASSACHUSETTS HISTORICAL SOCIETY

BIBLIOTECA NACIONAL, MADRID

MUSEO NAZIONALE ROMANO

UNIVERSITY OF MICHIGAN MUSEUM OF ART

COLLECTION OF CANDIDO GUINLE DE PAULA MACHADO, RIO DE JANEIRO

EGYPTIAN MUSEUM OF CAIRO

NY CARLSBERG GLYPTOTEK, KØBENHAVN

MUSEO ARCHEOLOGICO NAZIONALE DI NAPOLI

MUSÉE DES BEAUX-ARTS, NANTES, FRANCE

MUSEO DELL'ACCADEMIA, VENICE, ITALY

ARTHUR AND ELIZABETH SCHLESINGER LIBRARY OF THE HISTORY OF WOMEN IN
    AMERICA

NATIONALMUSEET, DENMARK

ALBRIGHT-KNOX ART GALLERY, BUFFALO, NEW YORK

UNIVERSITY OF CALIFORNIA, SAN DIEGO

GALERIE NATIONALE DU CANADA

McCORD NATIONAL MUSEUM, McGILL UNIVERSITY

RICHARD MERKIN COLLECTION, SMITHSONIAN AMERICAN ART MUSEUM,
    WASHINGTON, DC

RMN-HERVÉ LEWANDOWSKI, MUSÉE D'ORSAY, PARIS

BLACKBURN MUSEUM AND ART GALLERY, LANCASHIRE, UK

PENNSYLVANIA ACADEMY OF THE FINE ARTS, PHILADELPHIA

UWE SCHEID COLLECTION, MÜNCHNER STADTMUSEUM

STERLING AND FRANCINE CLARK ART INSTITUTE, WILLIAMSTOWN,
MASSACHUSETTS

JOSEPH J. PENNELL COLLECTION, UNIVERSITY OF KANSAS LIBRARIES

MUSEO E GALLERIE NAZIONALE DI CAPODIMONTE, NAPOLI

ASTOR, LENOX, AND TILDEN FOUNDATIONS

SCHOMBURG CENTER FOR RESEARCH IN BLACK CULTURE, NEW YORK

BIBLIOTHÈQUE HISTORIQUE DE LA VILLE DE PARIS

UNIVERSITY OF NEW MEXICO

NATIONAL ANTHROPOLOGICAL ARCHIVES, NATIONAL MUSEUM OF NATURAL
HISTORY, SMITHSONIAN INSTITUTION, WASHINGTON, DC

CHICAGO WORLD'S FAIR, 1893

GEOFFROY SAINT-HILAIRE AND FRÉDÉRIC CUVIER, HISTOIRE NATURELLE DES
MAMMIFERES

NEW ORLEANS PUBLIC LIBRARY

NEW ORLEANS MUSEUM OF ART SPECIAL COLLECTIONS DIVISION

UNIVERSITY OF WASHINGTON LIBRARIES

GEORGE EASTMAN HOUSE, ROCHESTER, NEW YORK

MANFRED HEITING COLLECTION, AMSTERDAM

COLLECTION PHOTOTHÈQUE DU MUSÉE DE L'HOMME, PARIS

ROYAL ANTHROPOLOGICAL INSTITUTE OF GREAT BRITAIN AND IRELAND

BIBLIOTHÈQUE NATIONALE DE FRANCE

WILSON CENTRE FOR PHOTOGRAPHY, LONDON

MENIL FOUNDATION, HOUSTON

MUSÉE D'ART ET D'HISTOIRE, GENEVA

WALTERS ART MUSEUM, BALTIMORE

MUSÉE NATIONAL DU LOUVRE, PARIS

MUSÉES ROYAUX D'ART ET D'HISTOIRE, BRUXELLES

MUSÉE D'ARCHÉOLOGIE BORÉLY

METROPOLITAN MUSEUM OF ART, NEW YORK

MUSEO CIVICO ARCHEOLOGICO, BOLOGNA

BROOKLYN MUSEUM, DEPARTMENT OF ANCIENT ART

STAATLICHE MUSEEN ZU BERLIN, ÄGYPTISCHES MUSEUM

BODE-MUSEUM, BERLIN

ORIENTAL INSTITUTE, UNIVERSITY OF CHICAGO

UNIVERSITY OF DURHAM, GULBENKIAN MUSEUM OF ORIENTAL ART

SUDAN NATIONAL MUSEUM, KHARTOUM

SAN QUENTIN PRISON, SAN QUENTIN, CALIFORNIA

CUMMER GALLERY OF ART, JACKSONVILLE, FLORIDA

DAVID & ALFRED SMART GALLERY, UNIVERSITY OF CHICAGO

SMITHSONIAN AMERICAN ART MUSEUM

YALE UNIVERSITY ART GALLERY

DALLAS MUSEUM OF ART

DAVIS MUSEUM AND CULTURAL CENTER, WELLESLEY COLLEGE

DETROIT INSTITUTE OF ARTS

FINE ARTS MUSEUMS OF SAN FRANCISCO

SMITH COLLEGE MUSEUM OF ART, NORTHAMPTON, MASSACHUSETTS

PALAIS LIECHTENSTEIN, WIEN

MUSÉE DES BEAUX-ARTS, CAEN

MUSÉUM D'HISTOIRE NATURELLE ET D'ETHNOGRAPHIE, LA ROCHELLE

MUSEO ARQUEOLÓGICO NACIONAL, MADRID

SIR JOHN SOANE'S MUSEUM, LONDON

STAATLICHE KUNSTSAMMLUNGEN, DRESDEN

CENTER FOR CREATIVE PHOTOGRAPHY, UNIVERSITY OF ARIZONA

ERICH LESSING CULTURE AND FINE ARTS ARCHIVES, VIENNA

FOWLER MUSEUM AT UCLA

ESTATE OF RICHARD SAMUEL ROBERTS

SEAN KELLY GALLERY, NEW YORK

CHARLES L. BLOCKSON AFRO-AMERICAN COLLECTION, TEMPLE UNIVERSITY

PAUL R. JONES COLLECTION, ATLANTA

HOLSINGER STUDIO COLLECTION, UNIVERSITY OF VIRGINIA LIBRARY

ARQUIVO NACIONAL, BRASIL

BENETTON'S CAMPAIGNS FOR RACIAL EQUALITY, 1989

ANDY WARHOL FOUNDATION FOR THE VISUAL ARTS, NEW YORK

AMON CARTER MUSEUM, FORT WORTH, TEXAS

MUSEUM OF CONTEMPORARY ART, LOS ANGELES

STONE TOWN, ZANZIBAR, TANZANIA

INSTITUTO MOREIRA SALLES, RIO DE JANEIRO

HISTORIC DEERFIELD, INC.

SAINT GERMAIN-EN-LAYE, PARIS

MUSÉE DE L'IMPRESSION SUR ETOFFES, MULHOUSE, FRANCE

MUSEU DE MARINHA, LISBON

MUSEU DE ETNOGRAFIA E HISTÓRIA DO DOURO LITORAL, PORTO

MUSÉE LÉON DIERX, RÉUNION DES MUSÉES NATIONAUX, SAINT-DENIS DE LA
    REUNION

MUSÉE NATIONAL DES CHÂTEAUX DE VERSAILLES ET DU TRIANON

EYES OF THE NATION: A VISUAL HISTORY OF THE UNITED STATES

III

Frame

There'd been a field, a farm, hobos asleep in a chicken coop,
white people whose dogs chased us every day on our way to the pool.
I never knew what, if anything, they grew. Never knew of a harvest.
Never saw a thing begin as seed, or sow its way to plant, flower, fruit.

There was a shack, I remember that, and an old house with an old lady.
She wore a dingy eyelet dress, and paced her porch dry
carrying a shotgun or a broom. Flip-flops, Blow-Pops, Click-Clacks,
Cracker Jacks, we barked Dog Talk with teeth still muddy and black

from Eat the Peg. Soft lime salamanders, fingers a vivid tangerine;
cow hooves grafted to arid grime; date palms with roots so determined
they sucked up all the water from the other things with leaves. We tore through her
property, a whole band of us, day after day, unaware of the endings

our bright forms would bring. There wasn't just one, but two
farms, across from each other, and another one, long down
the street, past the pool, next to the Victoria Park Golf Course,
where we never saw one colored man walk into.

Farther out, surrounding us, there were other farms too,
which had been worked, but were not working. There was the pool,
a liquor store, an old house, the golf course, a koi
farm, our new neighborhood, the bakery from Hawaii,

then the landing field for the Goodyear
blimp. You could live here for years and never
understand: Were you rural, industrial, or suburban?
We thought we were *home,* but our cardboard

was just slender venture on Negro sprawl.
Before that, it was law: we could not own property
except in certain codes: South Central, Compton, Watts,
where the construction companies were under contract

with the LAPD to tile or tar our addresses onto our roofs,
so when their helicopters needed to shoot,
they'd know—and we'd know too—
who was what and what was who.

Throughout the whole state, every third person
was from Lousy Anna: New Orleans,
Algiers, the West Bank, La Place, Plaquemines
Parish, Slidell, Baton

Rouge. We took pies and cakes to anyone new, but never heard
a sound from the farms. They never brought us nothing either.
No milk, eggs, no butter. It was just clear in the dirt
road we took. Somebody somewhere

was striding in time, but not any of us.
The farmers were lost
and hating it. We were lost
and couldn't care less.

The third farm I remember because I learned to drive in
it, just after they poured the cement, but before they painted the lines.
Shirleen down the street had it, a creamy sea-green 1969
Beetle. My sister was her best friend. Her baby sister was mine.

They were seventeen. We were twelve.
I'd practice in the evening, sitting on the crushed gold
velvet couch in our avocado green shag living
room. I pretended even then—even then—until I could feel it.

My majorette's baton became the stick shift,
cans of butter beans the brake, gas, and clutch.
The lesson came early, but I missed it: Ease
up when you let down, let down when you ease up.

Do both at once and you won't ever stall.
Choke that bitch if she don't start—
but choke her
sweetly. I remember when they first broke

the ground. It wasn't bigger than a four-car garage, but we only had one
car, so what did we know about how big a library was supposed to be?
It was the biggest any of us had ever seen—the only one
besides the three fragmented shelves

collecting dust in Detention Hall.
We'd hang off of each other, sucking the meat out of a giant
navel orange, tacky with juice and pulp, and watch
the corner of the old farmer's plot open up warm and ripe for us.

Trees felled, bush cleared, ground smooth. Small lathes of wood
the surveyor had joined with white string stood up straight in the red mud
whispering where our books would be. A neutral sky
blue, my first library card, my name in my hand—and typed!—

a first too. The lines of my alphabet so particular, so firm—
my definition now clearer than the Helen-Keller-mirror
in my parents' bathroom
(I liked the *R* most of all).

Then. So that I could see a photograph of an uncommon colored body—
besides a burnt body, or a bent body, or a bleeding body, or the murdered body
of the Reverend Doctor Martin Luther
King—Junior—

my mother ordered books, the kinds with immature
titles only the seventies could have produced:
Famous Afro-Americans, which had the same amount
of pages as Dr. Seuss.

Our textbooks stuttered over the same four pictures every year: that girl
in the foreground, on the balcony: black loafers, white bobby socks, black skirt,
cardigan, white collar. Her hand pointing. The others—all men—looking
so smart, shirt-and-tied, like the gentle men on my street, pointing

as well, toward the air—
the blank page, the well-worn hollow space—
from which the answer was always
that same hoary thud.

Every year these four photographs
taught us how English was really a type of trick math:
like the naked Emperor, you could be a King
capable of imagining just one single dream;

or there could be a body, bloody
at your feet—then you could point at the sky;
or you could be a hunched-over cotton-picking shame;
or you could swing from a tree by your neck into the frame.

Art & Craft

I would figure out all the right answers
first, then gently mark a few of them wrong.
If a quiz had ten problems, I'd cancel
out one. When it had twenty, I'd bite my tongue

then leave at least two questions blank: _____ _____.
A *B* was good, but an *A* was too good.
They'd kick your ass, call your big sister
slow, then stare over your desk, as if you'd

snaked out of a different hole. Knowing
taught me—quickly—to spell *community*
more honestly: *l-o-n-e-l-y.*
During Arts and Crafts, when Miss Larson allowed

the scissors out, I'd sneak a pair, then cut
my hair to stop me from growing too long.

Lure

I am not there

(We are not in that room.
I am not sitting on your lap.
I am not wearing the yellow
and white gingham skirt so pretty
Grandmother just made for me
this morning. Grandmother
is not sitting at her sewing
machine, revving the pedal hard
like an accelerator, driving herself
through the needle. You are not alive.
That fifth of whiskey is not empty
inside your pocket.

I am not three.
You are not seventy-nine.
Your fishhook fingers
are not toddling my birdseed
nipples over and over again.
I am not admiring the shine
of my new white patent leather shoes
resting at the edge of your knee.
Your other hand is not digging
inside my brand-new *Friday*
panties Aunt Lydia just gave to me
last week, because she was so proud
that instead of peeing in my diaper,
I'd learned to make it in the toilet. Grandmother
is not still sitting at her sewing machine, throttling
the pedal harder, louder. This is not your hand, your mouth,
your Pall Mall fingers, your fishhooks, your pearl-
handled switchblade. My father is not at work
mopping floors, unaware of me, sitting here
inside your lap. Alligator.

I am not three. I am not
breathing. I am not sitting in
your lap forgetting the body
has feet and legs and muscle
and sinew. And breath.
I am not just staring
at the wall.

Those are not your countless splendid
black bamboo fishing rods still hanging
upright out there on the garage walls.
Those are not the five gallons of salt
water sitting so still and pale
on the kitchen floor, the ones
we collected yesterday at the beach, to help
my sister's skin. We did not climb down
onto the giant rocks. Grandmother
did not tie pretty silk scarves under our chins
to cover our hair. We did not play
Hide-and-Seek with cranky blue crabs.
That beauty of a day never happened.
There is not a two-story giant avocado tree
in your backyard, whom I love more
than life. There is no grass, no
Pacific, no New Orleans, no Mardi Gras
stories for which I long, no boxes Mamere sends
each hot winter, filled with pralines and fudge
and purple and yellow and green plastic beads.
No Hail Mary blessed art thou amongst women—
I am not here.

My skin does not hurt.
My blood will not spill grey
anywhere. You will not find me
year after year. I will not ever remember
a thing. I will not stare at walls.
I will not see you, all my life, peering
at me from around random corners, whispering
something delicious out of a lover's mouth.

I will not dislike the feeling of touch, will not
be repulsed by the look of desire in an eye.
I will not allow my teeth to rot. The metal
implements of the dentist will not smell
sharp like fresh shucked pearls.

They did not send my mother away
when she was a little girl. They did not
put her on a Jim Crow train alone, in the middle
of a war, headed for Chicago, to make sure
you'd never touch her again, and again, for years.
You did not ever touch her again. They did not
not kill you. Again and again. They did not
not slice your body into fine brilliant offerings.

This is not that feeling that this is my body,
but I am somehow trapped inside
another girl, unable to say or feel a thing.
This is not the memory of another day.
I am not a wet headless footless squirming
thing you dug up from the dirt beneath the red
anthurium next to Grandmother's breathy
greenhouse and twisted onto a hook. I am not
a fresh pink pulsing thing splayed
on a tray my mother leaves
on your front porch
every Friday, dressed
so pretty. Violet. Hibiscus.
Red Bird. Of Paradise.
I am not there.
The air is not
frozen)

any longer.

The Body in August

Because when I was a child, God would pull me up into Her lap. Because when She pulled me up into Her lap, She would read to me. Because the story She read most was the one I liked least. Because every day She'd open that thin green book and say, This is the story of your life. Because, from beginning to end, there were only three pages.

I believe in that road that is infinite and black and goes on blindly forever. I believe crocodiles swallow rocks to help them digest crab. Because up until the twentieth century, people could still die from sensation. And because my hunger is so deep, I am ashamed to lift my head.

Because memory—not gravity—pins us to this trembling. And when God first laid eyes on us, She went mad from envy. Because if the planet had a back door, we'd all still be there—waiting for the air to approve our entry. Because your eyes were the only time the peonies said yes to me. Because no matter how many times I died, I always woke up again—happy.

Then, last night, after I'd yelled at him for the first time, my new son dreamt we went walking inside the trees. When we came across a squirrel, he said, I'd kicked it. Then the squirrel changed into a thin green book, which we read.

Because when God became a small child, I pulled Her up into my lap. Because when I pulled Her into my lap—to please Her—I opened my blouse. Because Her mouth is an impossibly pink place, a gaping raw cathedral, which She opened, teeth-to-nipple, then clamped down.

Second Line

for Henry Gabriel Lewis
& for Henri-Raphael Lewis

And then, one day, you fell and broke
your neck—just like that—while taking a shower.
Afterward, you walked back to your chair
and asked about the length and color
of the weather lady's skirt (It was brown).
When the ambulance arrived, you told them
Go on home. You were *fine.* Two hours later
you slumped over. Still, it took them three more days
to realize you'd severed your spine because the whole time
you told jokes and wouldn't quit smiling. *Pull my finger!*

Stoic and stolen so early on, what is it
about veterans of the Second World
War that makes Death require more convincing?
Three months in ICU, a broken neck,
three bouts of pneumonia, eight heart attacks,
a clement stream of steady infections, and yet
there you were—still: eighty-four, in a coma,
batting your eyelashes nonstop and full speed
at the world. Even while dying, you would
not die. So we were forced to kill you.
But then, we put on Ray Charles. And just when
they pulled the plug, he began your favorite song:
Hit the Road, Jack! Which you did. You hit it.
Before the song could end, you were gone.
I've never been so proud as I was that morning,
watching your breath Second Line home so quietly.

Except for that day when I first started
my period, and was ashamed. Nobody
would go and buy me anything because
they said it all came with the new messy
territory. But you drove me right up
to the store, said *Stay in the car,*
then came back out with a paper bag.

When you fell, it was the first month of spring,
March thirteenth. That day, I climbed up into the air
and could not climb back down until just now.

So how do you call that body born colored
and male, hunted and used for cog and prey?
Tree adornment? Altar cloth? War fodder?
And still—somehow—came laughter: often
and more eagerly than fear: your one half-good
eye forever fixed and cocked on the wry glint
of the world. When I was four, you showed me
how to play Tonk, and the proper way to throw down
a bone and score with sound. When kindergarten
began, they had to skip me two grades
because you had already taught me when
and how to Double-Down. That's what it felt like
to be Negro me, daughter of colored
janitor you: *pi* was not a pastry.
History was not a book. It was a smell
like damp cinnamon in your blue work shirt.
Starched pants. Union. Crawdad, crab-boil, oysters
shucked and soaking in their primordial
liqueur. It smelled like all of this, and the Vieux
Carré, its thick peculiar cotton air
breaking beneath the sea's sloppy
canopy. It smelled like the last high note
of the market woman's song-sing-song
whenever she cried *fresh strawberries!*

History was the smell of dirty whites
soaking in a hot tub of bleach; and
your first whore (that nice girl from Storyville
who Onc Félix took you to see when you
were a randy gentleman all of fourteen).
History was the morning of your first
communion; marbles and cigarettes pocketed
inside your muslin altar-boy gown;
it was the smell of gunpowder
from the small pistol you hid in your sock
(to protect your brother Lucien—and other
Negro doctor friends—while they tended
the colored Sick-and-Shut-In). It smelled
like a Palmetto tree, like every tree: red
with sap, warm with wonder; and holy
things, which are common and plain:
a brown paper bag; okra by the crate;
the ironing board when left in a room to cool;
my pencil you sharpened with your switchblade
each morning, just before I left for school.
I sensed all these things—the countries you'd seen,
but I had never been. I could smell the world all over you.
You gave it to me—a fresh, sharp walnut—pungent and coy.
You cracked it, plucked out its intelligence,
then dropped it in my hand: this deep black joy.

Pleasure & Understanding

Raga in an Afro-Dalit Bhava
Twenty-first Century

Lost landscapes within the body—haggard and lush terrains—
   North and South Poles suspended between pleasure and understanding.
Caravans, safaris, flask-filled hunting parties, all end in this solo expedition:
   you alone groveling from pleasure to understanding.

All is suffering is a bad modernist translation.
   What the Buddha really said is: It's all a mixed bag. Shit
is complicated. Everything's fucked up. Everything's gorgeous. Even
   Death contains pleasure—six feet below understanding.

Satiated, sweating, the monk lectures the whore,
   "Salvation comes to him who partakes not in sin."
"Well, it's a good thing I'm a girl," she replies, folding the damp bills
   between his pleasure and her understanding.

Politics, prostitutes, love—in that order. Never war's real horror. "Daddy,
   did you ever kill a man?" Dense silence. Then
tears so slow they never fell. Between us, this intricate moment
   electric with measured understanding.

I exist! I exist! I exist! grunts the ego, while the Self reclines
   on Her brocade divan, filing Her eighty fingernails.
With Her fortieth foot, She slides him a tray, and says: *Choose!*
   A chalice of pleasure, or a thimble of understanding?

Ancient rumor: When Marcellus captured Syracuse in 211 BCE,
  instead of destroying the city, he paused, and left
each building intact. It was said he believed it would reflect poorly
  on Rome were he to have destroyed *All this beauty* . . .

Your desire is like that, Thief: the perfect crime.
  You broke inside, but took nothing except
Pleasure's location within the Temple Understanding
  (But I wanted to be razed. I wanted to be plundered).

Sringaram—love; *hasyam*—laughter; *raudram*—fury; *karunyam*—
  compassion; *bibhatsam*—aversion; *bhayanakam*—terror;
viram—the heroic; *adbhutam*—wonder; in the tenth century, Abhinavagupta
  added *shantam*—peace. This is my two pence, *tamasha* notwithstanding.

The Lover takes ten steps forward. The Beloved takes fifty back. Sanskrit
  poems sing of how the rose trembles whenever the bee hovers near.
Listen, I have sobbed from pleasure. And I've cackled
  over my own tombstone, carved with: *Understanding*.

Ghazal literally means *talking to women:* a Persian form where royal men
  disguised their boy-love in song. We hide too, me and you.
The alphabet's our court. You're a Lady-in-Wading.
  I had a luxurious dowry—once—but now that measure's outstanding.

By the way, here's the page where I'd write you a love poem, if I knew
  anything about love—or poetry! <snort>
But I still remember—that sidewalk, that tree, that night—a tenderness
  so resonant (despite our imminent crash landing).

It doesn't matter who the *I* is, who the *you* is.
  You know who *you* are.
I know who *I* is. You're a Miss(ed) Pleasure—
  and I Miss Understanding.

But, for you, I wanted this to be a backyard swimming pool at dusk,
  lit from beneath—a thick palm above, lemon branches laden with apricot-
colored dates—a place for you to dive, head and hands first, spend the night
  backstroking between pleasure and understanding.

O Harbinger, what you bring is much more lush than spring.
  After the scarcest of light, Myth says you are the season's sign.
But I maintain you are a plea—something sure when we fall under—
  The Beloved's pulsing red reminder—always—to remain standing.

Félicité

for my mother,
and her mother,
and hers, ad infinitum

Of all three hundred species
    of hummingbirds, only one, the Ruby
        Throated, crossed

the Mississippi. Somehow
    this matters to me. They can hover
        in midair. They can fly

backwards. They fly
    five hundred miles straight
        through, across the Gulf

of Mexico without ever
    landing.
        Their mouths are hollow

burnished needles. Bright, sharp flutes.
    They sip the nectar of cactus
        flowers.

When "Louisiana" meant all the land
    from the Pacific
        to the Mississippi,

a grandmother of mine once owned one
    of the largest plantations
        in all the Territory.

When "Louisiana" meant Spain,
       she'd been a slave.
              When Spain sold itself back,

she's listed as the sole owner
       of a vast plantation—a plantation
              so large many property lines now form the boundaries

of an entire county.
       Tonight, after twenty-five years,
              I realized I've spent my entire life

avoiding any situation
       that might require me
              to say these words aloud.

From that moment
       I discovered her rotting inside
              a molding courthouse, her signature

next to the plantation's inventory,
       I began to babble
              any words I could think of

in four different languages,
       placing them in the most chaotic order
              possible, in order

not to say these words:
       The black side of my family
          owned slaves.

Or her signature: *Marie Panis,*
       femme de couleur
          libre—

Her lover
           was a famous judge
                     from Sardinia.

He took great pleasure
           in watching black women
                     hanged inside the Square

to musical accompaniment.
           I read this about him once,
                     then tried to see her,

brown, sleeping
           next to him, fucking him
                     on her plantation, on top of a pineapple

bed, kissing behind his ears
           sharing an alligator
                     pear, strolling

through her cane. Maybe
           at some point every hour
                     a part of me has wondered

about her—silently
           —though I did not think so
                     until just now.

Perhaps she is the answer
           to this sensation
                     I've had for years:

that of another body
           hovering inside me
                     waiting for address.

What can History possibly say?
           Sometimes I feel a pride I cannot defend
                     or explain. Sometimes I smile.

Into the barbed nectar
          of this story I have stared
                    my whole life.

Whenever someone tried to kiss me,
          I tucked her name under my tongue.
                    If someone tried too long

to hold me, I hid her between my legs;
          if they wanted to touch me
                    there, I'd pull out

her name and place the white bone
          under my pillow, hoping
                    she would return, take it

away, leave me
          a glistening
                    quarter.

To her son, Théodule, Marie Panis gave
          her "favorite" slave: a girl named Félicité.
                    They were married.

One of their children, Heloise,
          was my grandmother's great
                    great-great-grandmother.

There is a picture
          I found of her once, corseted
                    in a studio, standing next to a waist-

length pillar, which held a verdant fern.
          But mostly I have wondered: How
                    does one name a slave Happiness?

Happiness had a twin sister,
           Françoise. I don't know
                      what happened to her.

Perhaps, she is still
           out there, like us, her throat
                      glistening a silent red.

Or perhaps
           she is the only one
                      who can still cross the River,

the only one still flying
           backwards, over the Gulf
                      without landing.

Notes and Acknowledgments

NOTES

"The Wilde Woman of Aiken"

In 1882, Oscar Wilde toured the United States. Upon his arrival, many American critics, including comic-strip artists and photographers, chastised him for his theories on beauty. One photographer in particular, J. A. Palmer (Aiken, South Carolina), seeking to disprove Wilde's aesthetic—that anything could be beautiful—staged what he, Palmer, believed to be a satirical photo shoot, choosing objects he found to be inherently repugnant: highly patterned fabrics, an ornately upholstered chair, a sunflower, a face vessel, and a black woman.

"The Mothers"

This poem is dedicated—with love and gratitude—to the sublime memory of Gwendolyn Brooks, and to the occupants of her "Kitchenette Building."

"Let Me Live in a House by the Side of the Road and
Be a Friend to Man"

These poems are from an ongoing series in honor of the 1978 classic film *The Wiz*. Produced by Motown Productions and Universal Pictures, the film was a cinematic event. The first motion picture to be filmed at the historic Astoria Studios in New York, *The Wiz* was also the first U.S. film to include an entirely African-American cast. This series is dedicated to all those who participated in its production, most especially Lena Horne, Sidney Lumet, Geoffrey Holder,

Charlie Smalls, William F. Brown, Nipsey Russell, Ted Ross, Richard Pryor, Diana Ross, and Michael Jackson.

"Voyage of the Sable Venus"

"Voyage of the Sable Venus" is dedicated, with profound admiration, to the legacy of black librarianship, and black librarians, worldwide.

ACKNOWLEDGMENTS

Grateful acknowledgment is made to the following publications, where a number of these poems first appeared:

American Academy of American Poets Poem-a-Day: "Summer"
Callaloo: "Red All Over" and "verga:"
The Happy Hypocrite: "Félicité"
Lambda Literary Review: "The Mothers"
Los Angeles Review of Books: "On the Road to Sri Bhuvaneshwari"
Phantom Limb: "The Body in August," "Mother Church No. 3," and "Plantation"
Transition: "Frame" and "The Wilde Woman of Aiken"
Winning Writers: "Beauty's Nest" and "From: To:"

"Red All Over" subsequently appeared in *The Encyclopedia Project, Vol. 2, F–K,* edited by Tisa Bryant, Miranda Mellis, and Kate Schatz (Encyclomedia, 2010). "The Body in August" and "Frame" subsequently appeared in *Wide Awake: Poets of Los Angeles and Beyond, Pacific Coast Poetry Series,* edited by Suzanne Lummis (Beyond Baroque Books, 2015).

The following poems first appeared in these anthologies:

"Lure" originally appeared in *Cave Canem Anthology XII: 2008–2009,* edited by Randall Horton and Alison Meyers (Willow Books, 2012). Excerpts from "Voyage of the Sable Venus" originally appeared in *The Best of Kore Press 2012: Poetry,* edited by Ann Dernier (Kore Press, 2013).

"a dream of foxes"

in the dream of foxes
there is a field
and a procession of women
clean as good children
no hollow in the world
surrounded by dogs
no fur clumped bloody
on the ground
only a lovely line
of honest women stepping
without fear or guilt or shame
safe through the generous fields
—LUCILLE CLIFTON

with gratitude:

J. Bob Alotta, Dunya Alwan, Lee Azus, Rosebud Ben-Oni, Holly Blake, Janalynn Bliss, Pamela D. Bridgewater, Andrea Carter Brown, Vincent Brown, Sara Bruya, Tisa Bryant, Glenda Carpio, Ama Codjoe, the Coleman Family, Donna DeSouza, Kaila DeSouza, Denis Donoghue, Corinne Fitzpatrick, Jameson Fitzpatrick, Brian Francis, Jonterri Gadson, Chitra Ganesh, Helaine Gawlica, Hafizah Geter, Aracelis Girmay, Kimiko Hahn, Rob Halpern, Reginald Harris, Yona Harvey, Terrance Hayes, April Heck, Evelyn Brooks Higginbotham, Constance Vallis Hill, Page Hodel, Fanny Howe, Elisabeth Houston, Angela Jackson, Linda Susan Jackson, Madhu Kaza, Sara Kershnar, Mike Lala, Christine Larusso, Andrea Lawlor, Dorothy Lee, Helen Lee, Jordon Lee, Krishnakali Lewis, Vaishnavi Lewis, John Lucas, Ula Lucas, Kara Lynch, Kristin Maffei, Virginia McClure, JoAnne McFarland, Mary McHenry, Bernadine Mellis, Miranda Mellis, Julia Meltzer, Amina Meltzer-Thorne, Alison Meyers, Liz Miller, Jerome Murphy, Margaret Musgrove, Taura Musgrove, Alondra Nelson, Maggie Nelson, Marilyn Nelson, Mendi and Keith Obadike, Denise O'Malley, Greg Pardlo, Nina Payne, Geneva Perry, Kaye Perry, London Perry, Maya Popa, Carl Phillips, Toshi Reagon, Cat Richardson, Ed Robeson, Matthew Rohrer, Metta Sama, Kate Schatz, Nicole Sealey, Danzy Senna, Svati Shah, Charif Shanahan, Matthew Sharpe, Ellie Siegel, Michael Simonson, Tracy K. Smith, Adam Soldofsky, Anna Joy Springer, Louise Steinman, Zachary Sussman, Javid Syed, Nisa Tang, David Thorne, lê thi diem thúy,

Lynne Tillman, Jennifer Tseng, Steve Turner, Wendy S. Walters, Arisa White, Simone White, Dennis Williams, L. Lamar Wilson, Jenny Xie, Joanna Yas, Sarah Zapiler, and Rachel Zucker.

for the immeasurable gifts of both time and confidence:

The Headlands Center for the Arts, the Caldera Foundation, Summer Literary Seminars Kenya, the Ragdale Foundation. New York University's MFA writing community, especially Deborah Landau, Sharon Olds, and Yusef Komunyakaa, supported the writing of this book. Thank you, as well, to the USC PhD in Creative Writing & Literature Program, especially Percival Everett and Kate Flint. And most of all, to the inimitable Cave Canem Foundation, thank you: Toi Derricotte and Cornelius Eady.

and for all the love and faith anyone could ever need:

Elizabeth Alexander, Sheila Coleman, Alice Flaherty, Deborah Garrison, Judith Goldman, Adrienne Perry, Alice Quinn, Mala Rafik, Claudia Rankine, and Candice Watkins.

Finally, to my parents, Henry and Barbara Lewis, who committed the profoundly progressive act of taking a black girl's intellectual development seriously, I hope this book helps to repay the debt our society owes you and others like you. Thank you for convincing us—in spite of the world's lackluster narrative—that we were of interest and embodied a dynamic history.

Henri, you six-year-old wonder. Recently you said, "In the middle of Love Street and Heart Plaza, there's us." Thank you for choosing me.

Robin Coste Lewis is a Provost's Fellow in Poetry and Visual Studies at the University of Southern California. She is also a Cave Canem fellow and a fellow of the Los Angeles Institute for the Humanities. She received her MFA from NYU in poetry, and an MTS in Sanskrit and comparative religious literature from the Divinity School at Harvard University. A finalist for the Winning Writers International War Poetry Prize and the Rita Dove Poetry Award, and a semifinalist for the "Discovery" Boston Review Poetry Prize, she has published her work in various journals and anthologies, including *The Massachusetts Review, Callaloo, The Harvard Gay & Lesbian Review, Transition: Women in Literary Arts, VIDA, Phantom Limb,* and *Lambda Literary Review,* amongst others. She has taught at Wheaton College, Hunter College, Hampshire College, and the NYU Low-Residency MFA in Paris. Fellowships and awards include those from the Caldera foundation, the Ragdale Foundation, the Headlands Center for the Arts, and the Summer Literary Seminars Kenya. Lewis was born in Compton, California; her family is from New Orleans.

A NOTE ON THE TYPE

This book was set in Adobe Garamond. Designed for the Adobe Corporation by Robert Slimbach, the fonts are based on types first cut by Claude Garamond (ca. 1480–1561). Garamond was a pupil of Geoffroy Tory and is believed to have followed the Venetian models, although he introduced a number of important differences, and it is to him that we owe the letter we now know as "old style." He gave to his letters a certain elegance and feeling of movement that won their creator an immediate reputation and the patronage of Francis I of France.

Composed by North Market Street Graphics,
Lancaster, Pennsylvania

Printed and bound by Berryville Graphics,
Berryville, Virginia